MW00777308

Printed in the United States of America

First Printing, 2019

bbydoll press
Chicago, IL

www.bbydollpress.com

INTRODUCTION: ON TERMINOLOGY, AND OTHER [UN]IMPORTANT THINGS

Most of my scholarship, if you want to call it that, is located on various social media sites— mainly Twitter. I spend most of my days wrangling a defiant six year old and sitting at the computer, or on Twitter, producing content for my followers, and sometimes for myself. Sometimes it feels like what I do is of little importance. Sometimes it feels like I'm doing exactly what I was meant to do. Poverty is demoralizing, it robs you of the feelings of accomplishment you're supposed to feel when you do something great. It makes you question what "great" is.

What does it mean to be accomplished? Does it mean awards and accolades for everyone else to see? What counts as meritable? Am I a good writer if only ten or so people believe it to be so? Does my work mean anything if only my followers gas it? If, after I die, I am nothing but an old social media memory, did I even exist? What determines existence? Does one declare it vehemently, with every waking breath? With offspring, do we breathe life into the world, do we make ourselves again and again in order to extend our impact?

A former acquaintance once compared me to Maya Angelou. My writing is nothing like hers, but we do have erotic labor in common, like many creatives. Other than that commonality, it is a lazy comparison. People who have actually read my work compare me to Gloria Naylor and Zora Neale Hurston. I haven't gotten all the way into Naylor's work but I think the comparison to Hurston, might be apt. What I mean is that both of us did/are doing niche or innovative things to produce our work. Alice Walker said she discovered Hurston's name in footnotes in other folk's work, had to go digging for more information on a woman who had been long lost to many of us. Buried. Both inside and outside academia. Hurston traveled and collected information on various cultures, and she lived her experiences and died in poverty. That last part of her life haunts me. And I know she not the only Black woman this happened to.

I am haunted daily by my lack, and I hope to goodness that I don't die a footnote. I hope that poverty and lack of credentials doesn't smother me. Sometimes I feel like I'm being buried alive, choking, penniless. I'm spinning all of these words around but what does it all mean? People say all the time that I should be 'verified' [on Twitter], that I should be on bestsellers lists. That is not my measure of success. What success is for me, is food on the table. More babies, more love in my life. Money in my pocket to travel. Inches, of hair, and dick. And books, plenty of them, collected and written by me, for people like me.

I decided to start collecting my tweets and random essays just in case. I may lose my account, I may be erased from most people's memories. I will not presume that I am that important to you but I am that important to me. I am also aware that most people do not take the scholarship that is produced on Tumblr, Twitter, Facebook, and other social media platforms seriously. Real scholarship is in books, or comes from academia, or is recognized by hundreds of thousands of people. Until the right people have recognized me, I do not exist outside of my small social sphere. I started publishing things so that I could prove that I exist.

In this volume you will find an assemblage of Twitter threads and essays, proving that I did these things, proving that my lived experience, as well as my philosophies, are relevant. "what's in a name? thoughts on terminology & racialized slurs" was prompted by a few tweets on my timeline by white sex workers, who use the words 'ho(e)' and 'thot,' along with other popular Black slang terms, liberally, while denigrating 'survival sex workers' and thanking themselves for the charitable work they do for homeless or addicted prostitutes while proclaiming that they are "winning capitalism."

"Defined/Definers" goes further into terminology, questioning the strange binary of sex work/trafficking victim and the usefulness of the term 'sex worker' outside of a political context. After these two essays, I present a collection of Twitter essays of various lengths. I question if sex workers/erotic laborers are inherently revolutionary. I proclaim that money and intimacy go hand in hand. I ask that we discontinue the use of the term 'survival sex worker,' particularly in the pejorative sense. I wax on and off about undoing the notion of sex work and erotic labor issues as "single issue" in politics. I encourage feminists to look beyond choice feminism. I critique the "think about the children" dog whistle approach. Last, but not least, I examine current (Black) Black feminist attitudes toward erotic laborers and propose a proheaux solution.

I hope you enjoy this zine collection. My goal in the long run is to be able to publish other people's work. I also want to push people to take social media scholarship seriously. Strides have been made on Tumblr and Twitter, okur? One of my favorite scholars to read located her blog, Gradient Lair, on Tumblr. Together with Moya Bailey, Trudy of Gradient Lair helped develop the term misogynoir defined here loosely as: racialized misogyny targeting black women and girls. Her presence made me feel like I could create well-researched scholarship based in my lived experience— and I don't need a PhD to do it.

In the short run I will continue publishing my own work. I am a one-woman show over here, so it takes me a while. But the one thing I am is persistent.

--suprihmbé aka thotscholar

WHAT'S IN A NAME?
THOUGHTS ON TERMINOLOGY & RACIALIZED SLURS

I have several thoughts on the topic of naming when it comes to proheaux discourse. I am specifically saying "proheaux discourse" because, in my mind, proheaux discourse specifically speaks to Black/brown women and femmes and sex workers. When I say femmes I tend to mean all femmes, gender notwithstanding.

I. "SEX WORKER" VS. "PROSTITUTE"

The usage of the term sex worker versus prostitute is a point of contention I've noted. Colloquially, "sex worker" is used to mean prostitute/escort — a full service sex worker. According to the Introduction to the $pread Magazine anthology:

> "While it's contemporary, popular usage might suggest a polite synonym for "prostitute," its intended meaning is much broader, encompassing anyone who exchanges money, goods, or services for their sexual or erotic labor. The purpose of the term wasn't about being polite, although "sex work" does nicely sidestep the stigma embedded in some of the more charged monikers."

I, and other sex workers and/or sex worker activists, tend to use "sex worker" as an umbrella term. It's great for organizing, but:

1. Our discourse does not exist in a vacuum. The term sex worker is very much aligned in most people's minds as synonymous with prostitution. Whorerarchy dictates a severe pecking order, and listing "sex worker" in your bio automatically gets you the side eye because of this.
2. We also have to remember that "sex worker" is a political alliance, and that because of this whorerarchy, full service sex workers, particularly prostitutes and to a similar extent, escorts, tend to be the most vulnerable to assault and crimi-

nalization, with Black, trans, and indigenous sex workers as thee most vulnerable to murder, rape, and assault by police and civilians. This is why the movement tends to focus on full service workers to a greater extent. (In my mind it's similar to the WOC designation as political alliance, BW as a focus.)

II. ESCORT VS PROSTITUTE

An escort is an indoor prostitute. It seems fancier because it's dressed up. But just because it is in a hotel or someone's home, and not on the street or in a car, doesn't mean that escorts are any better than prostitutes who work on the street. Prostitute is a term used to describe full service workers at large but, really, it's a term used to pinpoint street workers. (Street work=outdoor prostitution, and escorting=indoor prostitution.)

I am not interested in respectability as far as this term is concerned. If an actual sex worker requests not to be called a prostitute, I definitely respect that. However, I find it distasteful that escort is being suggested as an alternative because the only difference between escorting and prostitution is perception. Although these two terms technically aren't racialized in the way that hoe and thot are, class and race in America tend to be inextricably linked, with whiteness positioned as the default. Being able to work inside is a privilege, especially for non-black and cis women. In certain areas, Black women and trans women are more likely to be targeted by hotel personnel and law enforcement, whether they are sex workers or not. Prostitution is linked to homelessness, and sex workers who work outdoors generally experience higher levels of criminalization and assault, not to mention exposure to the elements. (Note that runaways and children or others who have been coerced into street prostitution are not sex workers, but are affected by these issues as well.)

III. HOE, HEAUX, & THOT

When you say the words "hoe," and "thot," it's probably not a white woman you're picturing. That's because hoe and thot are Black American slang, sexual slurs usually reserved to name and shame Black women and girls of all ages, shapes and sexualities. From a very young age we are sexualized and stigmatized simply because of our skin. Thick and full-bodied Black women are made to feel like their bodies are inherently sexual, that [Black] men harass them because of "how they present themselves," placing the blame on them instead of the misogynists. The words hoe, thot, and heaux are rooted in cultural misogynoir.

White women's flippant use of these words has always made me feel some type of way, mainly because these words have been used to describe Black women/femmes since we were little "fast" girls. To see white women and white sex workers using all of these terms colloquially bothers me. While heauxdom is something a majority of them (and by them I mean able-bodied, cis white women) can dress to escape, Black women and femmes, whether cis or trans, civilian or sex worker, cannot escape these labels so easily. And white sex workers in particular grind my gears when it comes to discussing race, because many of them are so invested in feeling extra marginalized, and when Black and brown sex workers point out inequalities, we are either dismissed, talked over, or called "divisive." They don't like to think of themselves as oppressors (white) within an oppressed minority (sex workers).

I see Black women like me trying to reclaim the word "hoe" and its Frenchified sibling "heaux," and I wonder why white women, particularly working class white women, don't just reclaim a word that is actually relevant to them, like "slut?" Slut is also a racialized term, by the way, and it is a classist term. It calls to mind a lower class/working class white woman, i.e. "trailer trash." I also think it's very amusing, and telling, that the sexual slurs that usually describe white women are class-identified instead of race-identified. It speaks to the idea of whiteness as default. But whiteness can, and will, claim whatever it wants. Black slang is seaux trendy, ain't it? Our music, our language, is infectious and permeates every corner of the diaspora. Black culture and AAVE has always been fodder for white people, as have our bodies. I have found that cis white women who consider themselves to be part of an oppressed group beyond gender (i.e. poor/sex worker), or white women who have a certain level of proximity to Black people, either adopt a sort of off-brand, performative blackness, or co-opt Black slang and ex-

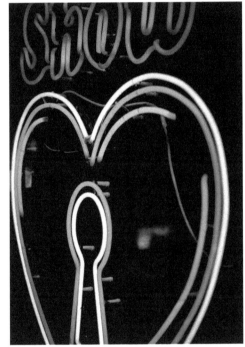

periences. Some will do this through cultural osmosis. Others will do it through their Black partner/friends/children/colleagues, and sometimes claim they experience racism by proxy.

I doubt that anything I have said here will prevent or dissuade white/non-black women or sex workers from throwing these terms around, nor was that my aim. I suppose I just like picking these things apart, and I don't generally expect people to change, least of all when that change would prevent them from doing what they want to do. Even as sex workers, white women have more power than Black women, and no one who has any kind of power is keen to give it up easily. A lot of folks will say "it's just words," but it's clear from what I've described, that these terms and the way in which we utilize them is important. Their connotations mean something, whether we wanna acknowledge it or nah.

NOTES:

1.   Despite there being a dearth of writing and work about Black sex workers by actual Black sex workers, ther are some academic pieces that I have enjoyed by Mirielle Miller-Young. Here's one: Putting Hypersexuality to Work: Black Women and Illicit Eroticism in Pornography. She mainly writes about pornography.

2.   Sinnamon Love is a retired Black porn actress you should look up. She had a piece in The Feminist Porn Book.

3.   I will definitely be searching for more Black sex worker blogs, art and writing, and I'll be doing a blog post on them!

TWITTER THREAD #1:

SOURCE: THOTSCHOLAR. (2019, APR 24). HOE IS NOT... [TWEET].
HTTPS://TWITTER.COM/THOTSCHOLAR/STATUS/1121234810624720896

1 "HO(E)" IS NOT FOR WHITE WOMEN TO RECLAIM.
2 "THOT" IS NOT FOR WHITE WOMEN TO RECLAIM.

3 RINSE AND REPEAT FOR "HEAUX." IT'S NOT FRENCH. IT
DOESN'T REFER TO WHITE WOMEN. YOU'RE NOT "THOT LEAD-
ERS." SOME THINGS ARE JUST NOT FOR YOU, AND THAT'S OKAY.

4 APPROPRIATING BLACK ENGLISH AND BLACK SLANG AND
THEN CALLING BLACK WOMEN'S USAGE OF CERTAIN WORDS
"MISSPELLINGS" OR "GHETTO" OR SPECULATING ABOUT THEIR
INTELLIGENCE DOESN'T COMPUTE. IT'S ANTIBLACK. STOP COLO-
NIZING OUR LANGUAGE AND REWRITING HISTORY.

5 YOU CANNOT BASH AND HARASS BLACK WOMEN AND BLACK
SEX WORKERS AND THEN USE OUR SLANG TO APPEAR TRENDY
AND EXPECT NOT TO BE CALLED ON YOUR BULLSHIT. ASK YOUR-
SELF WHY YOU FEEL SO ENTITLED TO OUR SHIT. WHY ARE OUR
WORDS "RATCHET" AND CLASSLESS ONLY WHEN WE USE THEM?

6 WHY DOES BLACK SLANG AND BLACK CULTURE ONLY LOOK
GOOD OR APPROPRIATE WHEN A WHITE PERSON IS DOING/SAY-
ING IT?

TWITTER THREAD #2; LAY LINGUISTICS, DIALECTICAL CROSSOVER, AND "HEAUX"

1 I HAVE LITERALLY BEEN UP ALL NIGHT TRYING TO DETERMINE THE ORIGINS OF THE −EAUX IN AAVE AND WHAT IT MEANS FOR THE WORD/TERM "PROHEAUX" OR "HEAUX." YOU'LL BE ASTOUNDED AT WHAT I FOUND.

*I AM NOT A LINGUIST. I DO NOT WANT ADVICE/FAUX EXPERTISE, I'M JUST SHARING.

2 FIRSTLY THAT UNSURPRISINGLY WHAT LITTLE I COULD FIND (AT FIRST) ATTRIBUTED THE −EAUX SUFFIX AS A LINGUISTIC FLUB OF SOME DUDE IN THE 1820S TRYING TO ANGLICIZE/SPELL FRENCH SURNAMES. OF COURSE THEY LINKED IT TO CAJUN−ACADIANS AND MADE NO MENTION OF CREOLE BLACKS.

3 SECONDLY THAT WE TEND TO LATINIZE/FRENCHIFY OUR "FANCY" ENGLISH WORDS−−ACADEMIC, SCIENTIFIC, ETC. ARE ALL FULL OF GERMANIC (NOUN)/LATIN (ADJECTIVE) DOUBLETS. THIRDLY, IM NOT ENTIRELY SURE IF I WOULD CONSIDER WHORE (HO[E])/HEAUX TO BE DOUBLETS BECAUSE IM

EXHAUSTED BUT I'M THINKIN.

4 FOURTH, I LEARNED THAT THERE ARE TWO OPPOSING SCHOOLS OF THOUGHT ON THE ORIGINS OF AAVE--THE CRE-OLE HYPOTHESIS AND THE DIALECT DIVER-GENCE HYPOTHE-SIS (OR ANGLICIST HYPOTHESIS). POLITICS ARE INVOLVED. I'M SURE IT'S PARTIALLY RACIAL IN NATURE. I THINK OF AAVE AS A DIALECT THO.

5 A DOUBLET (BTW) IS A PAIR OF WORDS THAT SHARE THE SAME ETYMOLOGICAL ROOTS BUT HAVE DI ERENT PHONO-LOGICAL FORMS

HO[E] (EYE DIALECTICAL AAVE FORM OF WHORE). EYE DIA-LECT IS BASICALLY SPELLING A WORD THE WAY IT SOUNDS. SEE: ZORA NEALE HURSTON

HEAUX: FRENCHIFIED VERSION OF HO[E].

6 THE -EAUX SUFFIX COMES FROM A BASTARDIZATION OF FRENCH BY CREOLE/-CAJUN FOLK. ADDING THE "X" AT THE END WITHOUT REGARD TO THE FACT THAT -EAUX IS A PLU-RALIZATION OF -EAU. IT'S MY THINKING THAT THAT SLIPPED FROM CAAVE/CE INTO AAVE. LIKE IT JUMPED DIALECTS.

7 SIMILARLY WE ALSO PROLLY HAVE CREOLE AAVE (AND MAYBE CAJUN FRENCH) TO THANK FOR THE WORDS BO-URGIE/BOUGIE/BOUJEE (DERIVED FROM BOURGEOISIE) AND BEAUCOUP/BOOKOO, TWO WORDS/TERMS USED OFTEN IN AAVE.

8 WHAT DROVE ME TO DO ALL THIS RESEARCH (THE SURFACE OF WHICH I BARELY SCRATCHED IN THREAD) WAS THE USE OR MISUSE OF THE TERM PROHEAUX BY SOMEONE EARLIER THIS MORNING (OR LAST NIGHT) IN A REPLY. I DIDN'T COIN THE WORD BUT THE TERM IS SOMETHING I'M DEVELOPING FOR BIWOC/BIPOC.

9 TRANSLATION: Y'ALL (NON—BLACK OR WHITE) CANNOT CO-OPT "PROHEAUX" AND USE IT AS A COOL NEW STAND IN FOR "SEX POSITIVE" BECAUSE YOU WANNA FEEL SUBVERSIVE/TRANSGRESSIVE. ISSA REAL THING BECAUSE I MADE IT SO.

Note: It is likely that there was some crossover between Cajun and Creole. I cannot be sure which culture originated the -eaux suffix on French (-derived) surnames-- they lived in such close quarters. I am not a linguist so I cannot comment in technical terms but I do know that the -eaux is from that area, came into general AAVE via regional CAAVE (Creole AAVE). The word "hoe," sometimes spelled "ho" is derived from the African-American pronunciation of "whore." "Heaux" is not plural, just as the surnames Devereaux and Breaux are not plural. Heaux is not French, either. It is wholly African-American, though Cajun-Creole derived. "Thot" is purely Black vernacular, an abbreviation of "that hoe over there." As these are part of the Black vernacular/creole, white Americans appropriation of these words is an extension of white supremacy. When we attempt to lay claim to these words among others, white people create their own criteria for who can say what words, even ones who agree. Instead of adjusting they become evangelists, because they must be centered always.

SOURCE: THOTSCHOLAR. (2018, APR 3). I HAVE BEEN UP... [TWEET]. HTTPS://TWITTER.COM/THOT—SCHOLAR/STATUS/981141389533642752

Twitter thread #3: engaging sex work as antiwork‡

1 Everyone wants to call themselves a sex worker, and everyone wants sex work to be WORK work, and I'm struggling to understand why. "Sex worker" is a political term, not some frivolous trendy phrase for y'all to throw on at your convenience, and "work" itself is terrible.

2 When I say "work is terrible" I'm speaking on work under capitalism. And because capitalism is compulsory, it's difgicult to engage almost any labor as symbolic of antiwork. It's almost impossible to opt out of capitalism/consumerism.

3 Like.... what do we actually *mean* when we say "sex work is work"? Are we attempting to normalize it? Are we aligning it with other types of work? Do we want to legalize it so that it is like other labor? Why do we pay taxes? Are we making a case for inclusivity?

5 My major question is: Can we move beyond "sex work is work"? Perhaps to engaging the phrase "sex work is (anti)work"? Past normalization? Or are there gonna be new edgy sex worker neighbors living across the street from Stan and Francine, loving in consumerism?

6 Favorite response/convo #1--the conversation was slightly derailed, but in a good way:

Quoted tweet:

I think it really depends on what you mean by (anti) work. anti-work as in non-productive work? I feel like that kind of work is tricky because productive/non-productive is a tenant of capitalism, and rejects the notion that non-productive

work isn't valuable.†

7 Favorite response #2:

Quoted tweet: I think sw is both work and anti-work. For me, that means that I want recognition that sw is just like physically a form of labor - that it's just as difficult and shitty and dignified and energy-expending as so much else that is called work - but simultaneously there is a trick §

Sources:

‡ thotscholar. (2019, Mar 21). *Everyone wants to call themselves a sex worker, [...]*

[Tweet]. https://twitter.com/thotscholar/status/1108729677928165376

† The_Erin_Black. (2019, Mar 21). I think it really... [...] [Tweet]. https://twitter.com/The_Erin_Black/status/1108743611275894784

§ MissLoreleiLee. (2019, Mar 21). I think sw is both... [...] [Tweet]. https://twitter.com/MissLoreleiLee/status/1108786738896486401

Twitter Thread #4: grey areas

1 anti-sex worker activists/fans weaponize sex workers negative experiences & sex trafficking victims trauma often to "prove" how damaging sex work is & why it needs abolishing, in the same way that anti-porn & anti-abortion activists weaponize the experiences of traumatized women.

2 there are sex workers who have been trafficked.
there are sex workers who have been pimped.
there are sex workers who have been assaulted.
some of them love their jobs.
some see their jobs as a means to an end.
some of them hate their jobs.
our exps often lie in a gray area.

3 this grey area is what i talk about in my space. i am one of the grey area sex workers who was assaulted, taken advantage of at times, and engaged in survival sex work at one (many) point/s before i had a kid. but i also like making my own schedule

4 the sex trafficking vs. sex work deal simplifies a very complex issue that 280 can't even begin to hack into. in sex work movement discourse we have our binaries:

sex work/sex trafficking
choice/coercion
consensual/nonconsensual
empowerment/violence
reality isn't this simple
5 this is why a lot of sex workers of color and poor sex workers feel alienated from both the sex positive feminist movement and the mainstream sex worker rights movements. emphasis on choice & empowerment

without an intersectional lens is an issue.

6 sex workers are not a monolith.

7 i think it's clear that we want sex workers who want to continue with their work to be safe & fully decriminalized, & i think it's also clear that we want more options for sex workers who do this work only because they lack other options. neither of these things is abt ur morals.

8 i think it's obvious that what makes sex work unique to other labor is that some of it is criminalized. removing that and other obstacles is a goal. many sex workers are anti-capitalist, tho they may or may not be Marxists, socialists, or communists. sometimes our goals align.

9 i think that sex work can & will exist in an anti-capitalist/womanist future for those who desire it and/or have use for it. porn, bdsm, massages, and prostitution for sure will never be eradicated, though other forms of sex work may change or die out as technology advances.

Source: thotscholar. (2018, Nov 5). anti-sex worker activists/fans weaponize sex workers negative experiences & sex trafficking victims trauma often to "prove" how damaging sex work is & why it needs abolishing, in the same way that anti-porn & anti-abortion activists weaponize the experiences of traumatized women [Tweet]. https://twitter.com/thotscholar/status/1059533589774262273

TWITTER THREAD #5: ON TERMS: "SURVIVAL SEX WORKER"

1 "Survival sex worker" is an ugly term, and I want to be rid of it.

2 From white sex workers weaponizing their "benevolent work" for "women who actually being raped and assaulted and getting pregnant by tricks and pimps," to academics juxtaposing it with "professional," I want us to burn this term in a dumpster fire.

3 As a BW who has worked on the street, in strip clubs, as a prostitute generally (offline, no ads or website), and has been assaulted and raped and survived domestic violence, I find it exhausting/telling that I must list my trauma in order for my knowledge to be taken seriously.

4 I have been working since way before FOSTA/SESTA. I took some breaks in btwn, as we all do, but I have been in and out this shit since I was an old 17-18 years old. Never considered myself a "sex worker" till recently--it's a white/classed term tbqh.

5 I didn't get really active online till 2010. I didn't get on Twitter till 2013, and I didn't start tweeting actively until 2016. I had 600 followers then. But now, suddenly, I'm popular because I'm Black and white people like me, and all my experience is thrown out of the window.

6 I'm rambling, but going back to my first tweet, we are all working to survive to some extent. Recently, more and more people have been relegated to part time/temp work *globally*, and more and more of us are engaging in freelance or piecemeal work to survive.

7 So, in a greater context the term "survival sex worker" is often being used to class drug users who are street workers, women who may or may not have experienced homelessness or (sexual) violence. I'm being located outside of that because I have a Twitter.

8 The term "survival sex worker" is assigned to these groups by sex workers arguing about who gets to be a ho(e) who don't see the classism inherent in assigning a term to a group they don't consider themselves a part of, & listing trauma as criteria.

9 I'm tired of y'all using and weaponizing "survival sex workers" to concern-troll online-- all so that you can shut a Black sex worker up and dismiss my work because you don't like what I'm saying about race/class. Or so you can prove what a good person you are.

Source: thotscholar. (2019, Apr 25). "Survival sex worker" is an ugly term, and I want to be rid of it. [Tweet]. https://twitter.com/thotscholar/status/1121514655128616961

TWITTER THREAD #6: NOT DEBATEABLE

1 When you center morality in your quest to denounce sex work and sex workers you are in fact creating and encouraging a climate in which poor people, and the ways we survive and outsmart structural oppression, are rendered "immoral."

2 I am not an empowered sex worker. I am not a "survival sex worker" either, as that phrase is often juxtaposed with "professional sex worker" and I have no time for that. I am a person who has traded sex both as my primary and secondary/supplemental income.

3 Y'all make a lot of things that involve sex or poverty about morality, so trading sex is doubly vile to y'all, & is a "vice" along with running/doing drugs, gambling, and other pleasurable things that get poor people jail time and rich (white) people sympathy. Whose morality?

4 Anyway, trading sex for money has enabled me to (mostly) avoid homelessness, provide for my kid and myself, buy food, create this platform so that I could do what I really wanna do, which is: be an artist. Creatives have alway been whores or whore-adjacent. Look at blues singers.

5 As a kid I loved blues singers and fell in love with the Jazz Age. Here were these poor Black artists making a way in a world of vice. Doing drugs. Fucking. Doing queer shit. Brothels. Buxet flats. Speakeasies. Hairstylists. Gamblers. Whores. Hustlers. Writers. Poets. Dancers.

6 There is nothing immoral about poverty, and I am honestly not here to prove that trading sex is moral because what do I care about your morals? Morals are manmade and in flux, but my right to fuck who, how and for what I want and to survive on this earth is not debatable

TWITTER THREAD #7

3 Survival sex workers would be [considered] members of the under-class. This is where they throw informal laborers, under- or unemployed laborers--those who cannot or are not willing to work or have never worked. Sociologists separate the underclass from (poor) working class.

4 Coming full circle you have these "hoe is life" Black women who may or may not identify as feminists, latch onto "men are trash" and who reclaim (racialized) gender-based slurs and certain pro-sex politics or phrases without unraveling their hatred/dislike of erotic laborers.

5 There is a lot of reductive or half-ass arguments going around based on this sex strike convo that I'm tryna probe. I think lots of folks also reduce "all women are whores" from its hyperbolic, yet truthful roots: gender-based oppression based in sexual-reproductive control.

6 I find it strange that I haven't seen many Black repro justice activists connect more to the politics surrounding erotic labor that are definitely connected to control of reproduction and related activities (sex). I'm not saying no one has done it. I'm saying it's not prevalent.

7 I personally believe that respectability is what is preventing Black women and feminists/womanists from fully untangling their issues around sex work/erotic labor. Marriage, cheating, sex strikes… same convos again and again, and they have barely changed.

8 Respectability isn't the only thing stopping these convos from moving forward though. Classism w/in the Black community is a thing. In our community sex workers/erotic laborers are often classed as underclass. That is exactly what is evoked when folks say "survival sex work/er."

9 The term "survival sex worker" is used as a catch-all identifier and it often creates a specific (often racialized) class of sex worker. Survival sex workers, then, are not only classed as a below-working class (underclass) but are also juxtaposed with "professional sex workers."

10 I'm being somewhat brief because I'm summarizing my thoughts atm. But I think in order for BW and feminists/womanists convos around sexual politics to move forward we need a proheaux womanist lens--a discourse that centers the politics of erotic labor rather than ghettoizing it.

Photo by Terry Vlisidis
thotscholar. (2019, May 13). Survival sex workers would be members of the underclass… [Tweet]. https://twitter.com/thotscholar/status/1128004754087600133

TWITTER THREAD #8: SEX STRIKE

most sex strike discourse is cissexist/heterosexist and ignores the fact that sex isn't important to everyone, including men. it also centers sex as the most important thing to men-hypersexualization. and it's not a long term solution nor a solid solution to systemic issues.

Quoted tweet:

*SEX STRIKE:
Someone asked me my thoughts on sex strikes today, so what do you all think about them? I want to hear from Black women and femmes mostly, but if anyone else wants to answer that is fine too. (I'm also considering labor and also pleasure)

Sources:

thotscholar. (2018, Aug 3). Most sex strike discourse... [Tweet]. https://twitter. com/thotscholar/status/1025483574332542976

*ZalUlbaorimi. (2018, Aug 3). SEX STRIKE... [Tweet]. https://twitter.com/ZalUIbaorimi/status/1025480731638804481

Defined/Definers
*My thoughts on common terminology around erotic labor &
trafficking*

Introduction

There's an ongoing debate about terms within and without the
so-called community of erotic laborers that I find both frustrating
and interesting as a person who has straddled the lines of advocate and prostitute off and on for almost a decade. I have worked
in many areas of what allies, "abolitionists," researchers, and sex
worker rights activists call sex work. I only recently began using
the term sex worker to describe myself because I found it helped
the right people find me, and vice versa. I am highly aware that
most sex workers in my tax bracket do not use this term to describe
themselves, so I am often wary of employing this term in everyday
conversation, and I struggle to find terms that suit the needs of the
women around me. I say women because my work mainly focuses
on cis and trans women of color, and comes from my perspective
as a queer Black cisgender woman who is a self-defined sex worker. I have engaged in several areas of "the trade," from stripping
and street prostitution to camming and phone sex, and what some

might call "companionship," aka indoor prostitution. Here is a short, but not exhaustive, list of some of the various professions and terms we use to describe ourselves:

Escort	(Exotic) Dancer
Street-worker	Stripper
Hustler	Sugar Baby
Companion	Erotic Laborer
Prostitute	(Web)camgirl/camboy
Hooker	(Web)cammodel
Hoe/Heaux (racialized: Black vernacular)	Whore
	Performer
Slut (racialized: white, but not exclusive because reverse racism doesn't exist)	Sex Worker

Usually when I speak to other women in similar lines of work they do not use the term "sex worker" to describe themselves, though I will use it throughout this article to describe this amalgamation of diverse individuals. Many struggle to define what they do as work because in American culture work is defined as "labor performed legally in exchange for money" (Susan Dewey & Tonya Germain 2016). So despite the fact that our work is labor-intensive and time-consuming, very few of us see it as legitimate labor. Why would we when many of us are engaging in sex work purely to survive, in a country that denigrates feminized labor as a rule?

I have often likened sex work to what Dewey and Germain termed "service sector work," especially the most feminized areas such as housekeeping/cleaning, food prep/cooking, caregiving, and other forms of domestic work. These are all areas that I have worked in, and they all feature jobs that provide little to no benefits, have low pay and rare pay increases (and even those are low), and offer little room to adjust your work schedule. I worked at a hotel in Milwaukee from April 2009 to April 2010. The reason I had gotten into stripping and dipped into street work and occasional hotel/motel prostitution was because I couldn't find a "regular" job to pay my bills. I applied for several jobs and went on interviews, but it was a small, racist college town and nobody was checking for me. With my back against the wall I applied at the only strip club in town and got to working. I danced 50+ hours per week just to get by. When the money dried up, as so often it does, I "prostituted" myself fully, for the first time (and a large sum of money--in my mind), and got the hell out of Bloomington.

Strangely, I did consider what I was doing to be work because I defined work as "something that gets me money to pay the bills on a regular basis." However, I was hyperaware that other people looked down on my kind of work. If you had asked me then what I was doing to get by I would have answered the same as any other young Black woman: hustling. "Dancing." I never told anybody I had been fucking for money until I joined groups on Facebook.
The work I was and am doing is widely considered immoral both culturally and religiously. At eighteen I was ashamed. At nineteen I began to wonder why I was ashamed. I had been reading bell hooks and Black feminist work that was anti-porn, and as a young skeptic I often found myself questioning or in disagreement. My complaints were, and are, often met with anger, deflection, or ridicule. How dare I disagree with my (better educated or reasonably established and revolutionary) Black feminist foremothers?

At that young age I didn't know enough to disagree with purpose and persuasion. So I read, and I disagreed inwardly, until I found the words I needed to articulate what I meant, so that I could out-inform everyone who came at me sideways.

On Carol Leigh's "sex worker" and the invisibility of Black sex workers

Over time my language has shifted. Even in the past year I have questioned my and others use of certains words and terminology to describe what "we" do. I have had to adjust to accommodate varied perspectives of women like and unlike me who struggle and straddle the lines (or lie on the spectrum) between what so-called abolitionists and sex worker feminists have termed "sex work" and "sex trafficking." I have had to ask what it means to legitimize my and others labor, what to call myself, how to describe these issues in a multicolored way. How to globalize my perspective to include my indigenous diasporic sisters. How to respectfully dissect and deconstruct the racialization of the term "indigenous" and ask why it isn't often applied to my African siblings. How to express my needs and take in concerns about the needs of others. What is consensual? What is coercion? How to self-define in a world where I am not seen as a definer by definition. Most of these words or terms have been used in a derogatory way or to insult non-sex working cis and trans women, particularly Black women.

So what does this mean in the grand scheme of things when we are struggling to form coalitions and communities around these politics? There are researchers, academics, and white women classed above me who are giving lessons on terminology and using the words "consensual," "empowered," and "choice" to comment on what constitutes "sex work" and what is "sex trafficking." This is really the crux of the issue. The two main reasons that this conversation is not being had more widely is 1) because the sex worker movement is dominated by white women who are usually better off than me or academics and researchers who feel they set the standard for the rhetoric/theory surrounding our issues and, 2) because we lack a clear intersectional politics that firmly decenters whiteness and wealth. The latter is what I am trying to help remedy with my politics of proheaux womanism that is geared specifically toward Black and Brown erotic laborers and can be utilized by allies and nonblack sex workers to gain insight and understanding.

There are many who have argued that we should strike the words "prostitution" and "prostitute" from our wider vernacular and that we should use the terms "sex worker" and "sex work" as a rule. I am not always sure how I feel about this. The word itself is useful, same as queer, but it doesn't work as an umbrella term for obvious reasons. However the suggestion to use a "better" term, smells of respectability politics to me, and that's grody. I don't think the wording matters so much as the context, since it was outsiders who made the term prostitute derogatory in the first place, by denigrating the profession and its subjects. Feminized work is derided by the general populace. Note how service work is not considered career work unless one is in a position of power. "Sex work" caught on in research and academia and the trickle down effect has been for them to turn around and tell others: "This is what you call them now." Yet when Dewey and Germain went out into the street, they said the women were offended by the term and many preferred to call their labor "hustling."

Sometimes I refer to the "law" of self-definition. But what does all this mean when we are trying to convene under one umbrella? I call myself a proheaux womanist which is my own invention and has more to do with politics and turning theory into praxis for a wider group of (Black and Brown) people. Most people involved or interested in our politics use the term "sex worker" which was coined by Carol Leigh aka Scarlot Harlot, a white woman and prostitute activist. White women of all social standings have already begun their appropriation and co-optation of Black vernacular terms such as "hoe/heaux" and "thot." I sometimes fear that in our quest to protect and connect we are removing vital descriptive language. The point of language is efficiency and understanding. Will we ever come a to consensus on what terms to use to further our cause?

In her book *Funk the Erotic*, L.H. Stallings suggests engaging sex work as a form of antiwork, which I and many other erotic laborers have directly and indirectly determined to do via our critiques of capitalism and labor. She calls this "transing" sex work theory. She writes that "trading sex and sexual culture in black commu-

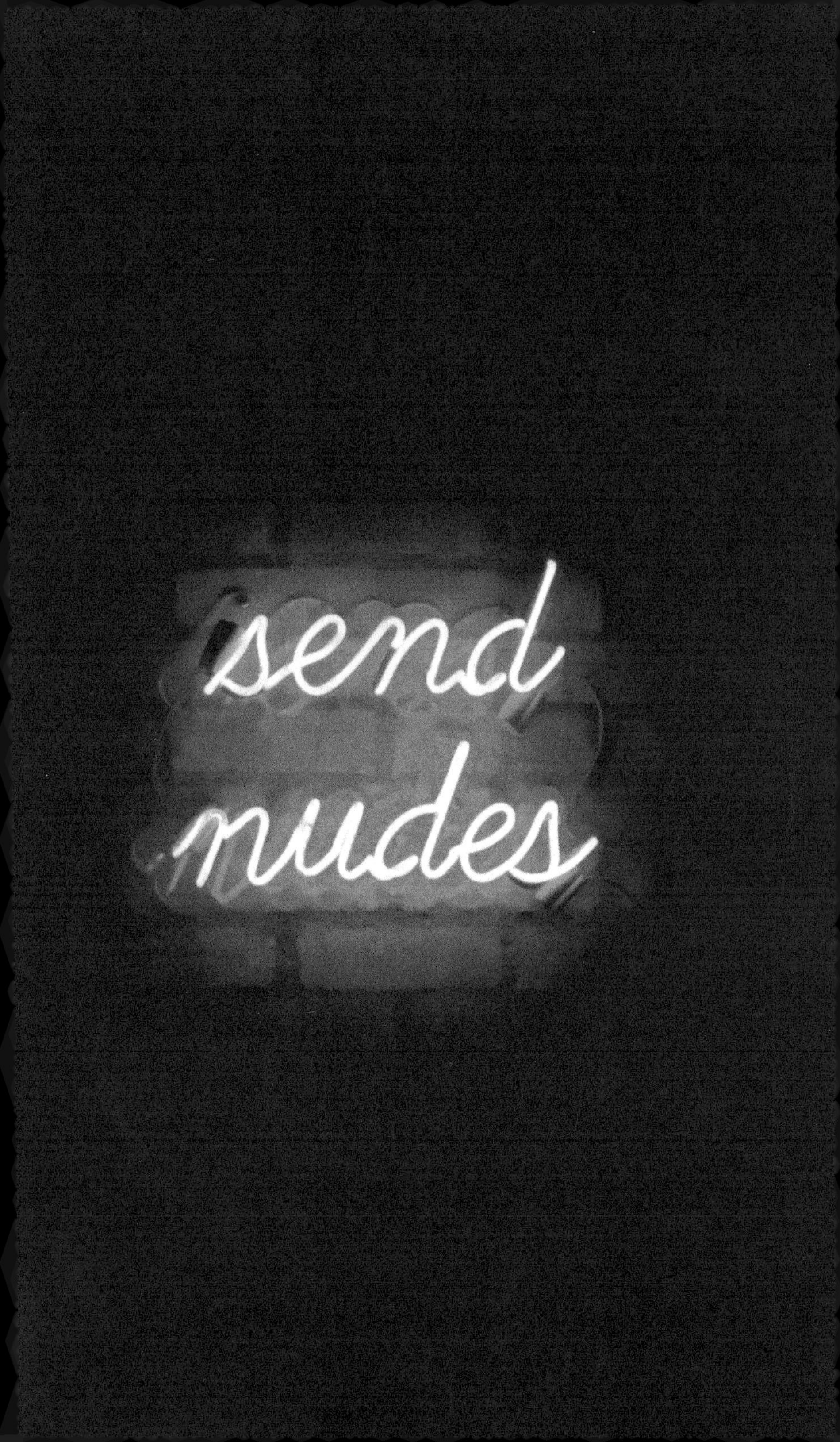
send
nudes

nities had already been conceptualized as postwork imagination."
This part of her work is interesting to me. It is also interesting to
see how other Black people, Black women in particular, not in my
social position but above, see me and my (anti)work. Later in the
same chapter and section Stallings writes: "Instead of beginning
from the position of the state and entity that implicitly gets to au-
thorize and define what constitutes sex work, even as the term was
created by prostitute activists reacting to state policing, we should
all reconsider and rethink the term and meaning with questions
such as: Why is it that the only individuals classified as sex workers
are those whose labor is connected to sexual pleasure?" (Stallings
2015)

I love the phrase "prostitute activists" but part of me feels like this
question answers itself, and that (perhaps) there is an implicit bias
that drives Stallings to want to push the term "sex worker" to its
limits to include researchers/academics and others as sex workers
in order to supposedly broaden the community and support. Or
perhaps I am the one who is biased—I am very protective of my
space and I feel like the more we stretch the term "sex worker," the
more prostitutes and erotic (porn) performers become decentered,
even obscured. I feel like the constant attempt to push the term
sex worker to its limits to accommodate those who feel "left out"
does not acomplish anything materially—nor do I think we should
water-down the term sex worker to rope in academics who write
aboout sex— academic writing aboout pornography differs greatly
from erotica which is designed to titillate. Though I am skeptical
of certain aspects of identity-based politics (i.e. weaponization of
identity in order to avoid accountability or using identity to de-
fame someone as part of a personal grudge), I believe that any re-
consideration of the term should be led by sex workers, and the rest
should follow.

However, the push from many other erotic laborers to switch from
"prostitute" to "sex worker" and other more palatable terms begs
the question: Who gets to define what? Who or what is a sex worker? Will "sex worker" become thee respectable term as folks deem

the words we call ourselves derogatory and correct others without reference? Does "sex worker" even apply when many (Black and Brown and poor) erotic laborers reject the term entirely? (I do not use the term outside of organizing and political work.) This is the hard work of building and maintaining community which is a multitude of multiply marginalized communities, and of developing a language and discourse that encompasses a variety of experiences and not just a select few or the (white) majority.

It is also not lost on me that there seem to be very few Black erotic laborers outside of academia whose words or work is actually cited, or even known. There's seems to be a dearth of recognized critical and practical theory being created by Black former and current erotic laborers. I wonder if this is because white sex workers have done a better job at documenting their work, or if their work is simply more widely known and accepted in academia, or if its because many of the names we do know are women who have degrees—Carol Leigh, for example, has a degree in criminal justice. Siobhan Brooks, a former Black stripper of the famed Lusty Lady who is the author of *Unequal Desires: Race and Erotic Capital in the Stripping Industry*, has a bachelor's in women's studies and a PhD in sociology. But really, there are not many women like me whose experiences are recorded.

Where are the books that engage Black erotic laborers direct lived experiences, as well-rounded characters in our own narratives? Where is the creative work that centers philosophies and culture that I know we have created? It is my goal to find and record these hoe histories, as I have termed them.[1]

what "consensual" means

Consensual. That's the word I keep seeing on my timeline as I flit from tweet to tweet examining the politics of my peers. Sex work is consensual. That's what makes it different, supposedly, from sex trafficking. I used to say so too, though when I would read and talk

and probe I would ask myself what I meant. Much of the time my experiences with erotic labor straddled the make-believe line between consensual and coercive, in both an economic and physical sense. I remember quoting someone in a tweet (now deleted) that said something like "nonconsensual sex work is an oxymoron." That's ridiculous, right? When I was pushed to dig deeper into my language I knew exactly where that line of thinking fit, and it's an area I try to stay far away from—"higher-calling discourse" (Heather Berg 2014). In trying to stop the person from conflating sex work and sex trafficking I ended up erasing, not only other sex workers who have experienced trauma or came to the profession via trafficking or other coercive methods, but myself. These are the key binaries:

Choice/Coercion
Voluntary/Involuntary
Consensual/Nonconsensual
Professional/Survival

I have experienced lots of "nonconsensual" moments while engaging in various modes of erotic labor, where I have consented to one thing and have been pushed into doing another, either by a person or by individual circumstance ("I needed the money"). Once you are in the room or in the car your options are limited--you are the one who will be arrested and possibly assaulted or raped by law enforcement should you get caught up. There are people who have been trafficked and forced into sex work. There are sex workers who have been assaulted/raped while on the job. There are people who emigrate to America and are forced into domestic work or other exploitative situations. There are people in this country who are forced into the sex trade by family members or other trusted adults, partners, or caregivers, and who later choose sex work as a means of income and/or survival. What we need to do is acknowledge that, even though there are some people who have been forced into sex work or other types of exploitative work, they still deserve consideration. People who trafficked into sex work are no different from people who were trafficked and forced into sweatshops, or those who are migrant workers/sharecroppers. Capitalism has driven many people into work they would never have considered before and strutural oppression and, particularly in the case of erotic labor, laws created that constrict ad impose upon independent movement and encourage exploitation by third-parties, force people into exploitative situations.

I chose to become a stripper out of necessity. I needed money. As a stripper I had to pay all sorts of unregulated fees to work at the clubs I worked at. Clubs are allowed to make up their own rules within the bounds of state and federal laws, which are not necessarily favorable to the dancers. The laws vary from state to state. Each club also has its own set house fee and tipping requirements. The strippers pay everyone else out of the money they earn. There are very few stripper unions. Whose favor is this in? Obviously the strip clubs. Yet women continue to choose to strip. Some of the women are just looking for thrills. But many of the women who choose this and other kinds of work are poor and thus easily exploited. This is true of housekeeping, stripping, and most forms of feminized labor. If we complain about work conditions it goes back to "you signed a contract," which implies that our work is consensual. This is a huge problem with the language of consent.

Calling all sex work consensual or voluntary as a rule means that any negative interaction while sex working that is non-consensual will either be lumped into sex trafficking (which will probably involve state intervention and/or removal of or disregard for agency of the subject) or it be will written off as "stolen goods" or the perils of the job. This is a way that the language of "choice" is used against us. It becomes more dangerous when you factor in rape culture and the politics of consent, and disingenuous when you factor in class. Consent is an ongoing process, and once you start saying things like "actual sex work is consensual" you are wading into dangerous waters and running the risk of erasing a large demographic within the community. When I was being harassed people asked me why I chose such a dangerous profession. When I ask(ed) for money even certain Black feminists suggested low-wage service jobs, as if I have never been or wouldn't be sexualled harassed or assaulted in those professions. They suggested putting my son in public school, as if I don't have valid reasons for homeschooling. If I decide these suggestions are not suitable for me, they become exasperated and say "You're basically choosing to be ____."

On the uselessness and redundancy of the term "survival sex worker"

Another language problem we have is centered around the term "survival sex worker," which has become a catch-all term for poor and working class erotic laborers who may or may not be homeless or home-insecure. The term *survival sex worker* is a wholly unecessary term used to group together "low end" sex workers who are not making a living wage. It is a term fraught with stigma that borders on the pejorative, especially when used by people who are not members of this class of sex workers. Indeed, "survival" evokes an image of a poor, possibly drug addicted, prostitute who most likely works on the street or out of strip clubs or Backpage mimics, and is working to make ends meet. Although we already have adequate terms to describe these groups of sex workers (poor/working class, drug addicted, homeless), *survival sex worker* has become the term du jour to group together these varied demographics and set them apart from "high end" prostitutes and other erotic laborers who more often call themselves "providers," "companions," and "escorts," when they are not appropriating racialized/classed vernacular for cool points on social media (i.e. hoe, heaux, thot, slut, etc.). Provider, companion, and escort are euphemisms, marketing tools, used to set oneself up as "high end"—luxury. As I stated in a previous piece, "[a]n escort is an indoor prostitute." In contrast, *survival sex worker* tends be utilized as a euphemism for street workers, or for poverty-stricken, struggling prostitutes/erotic laborers. Though there are many escorts, companions and other so-called high-end prostitutes who are struggling financially or with drugs (esp. due to racial capitalism and body politics), only poor, homeless, and working class erotic laborers are given this title meant to denote that they are struggling in a unique way. This sets up a hierarchy wherein other erotic laborers, as well as non-sex workers, are able to exercise their savior complex and set themselves apart from "survival sex workers" in the same way that middle-class people generally set themselves apart from impoverished people. Not only that, *survival sex worker* as a term separates poor erotic laborers from other poor people and partially obscures the fact that coercion via capitalism is something we all experience to varying degrees. There is no equivalent term for upper income erotic laborers.

I have witnessed people juxtaposing survival/professional erotic labor as if these are two distinct groups. For many the point seems to be to capture that grey area between sex work and sex trafficking, but the term *survival sex worker* fails at this, instead promoting a dichotomous image of disempowered low-end erotic laborers who are simply 'surviving', and 'empowered' high-end erotic laborers who are looked at as astute, capable businessfolk. This mirrors our culture's feelings about poor people, as well as reinforcing the choice/coercion binary. It is implied that those who are just "surviving" are making poor decisions, are drug addicted, or were coerced into the work, economically or otherwise, in a way that most 'empowered' sex workers are not.

I fit the demographic the term *survival sex worker* is meant to describe. I am a struggling, impoverished erotic laborer and mother of one. Up until the end of 2017 I was living with family or else struggling to keep an apartment of my own. I have never made a living wage. I engage in several different forms of hustling to make ends meet. I am a writer, artist, editor, publisher, orator, phone sex operator, sometimey cammodel, former and current (if it suits me) prostitute, and organizer. I pay taxes. I manage my own businesses. Am I not professional? "Professional" itself is an ambiguous category—the standards are arbitrary and vary from company to company, person to person. Yet, the term used to describe someone like me who is poor and an erotic laborer is "survival sex worker." The word "professional" has synonyms such as *skillfull, adept, expert, seasoned, and bussinesslike*, in contrast with antonyms *amateur, layman, incompetent, unskillful, and inept*. Poor: destitute, impoverished, low, poverty-stricken, needy, inadequate.

One might describe a "professional sex worker" as one who works full time, is an "expert," and performs skilled emotional and physical labor, and pays their taxes. One might say that a "survival sex worker" is one who is defined by their inability to make a liveable wage, who is unskilled, or is mainly working to get the job done, implying a lack of effort or perhaps a lack of agency or business acumen. The term *survival sex worker* reinforces the notion that poor sex workers are not as skilled as upper income erotic laborers, which couldn't be further from the truth. Why do we continue to utilize this term? I believe it is because of who dominates the current discourse.

Survival sex worker also obscures the fact that there are erotic laborers of all income levels who got into the profession because they needed the flexible work in order to accomodate chronic illness, disability, or lack of affordable childcare. Not all of these people are labled "survival sex workers" but they are certainly working for survival, right? Why then do we continue to employ this classist, nebulous term to denote who is and isn't working for survival? Survival implies a dire state, it is a word fraught with drama and implications of trauma. Why don't we just say exactly what we mean? These are specific words and groups that are already part of the dominate vernacular. We already have words that describe our distinct needs. The point of (my) proheaux womanist scholarship is to break with these binaries, and that includes vague, derogatory terms like this.

Works Cited

Berg, Heather. "Working for Love, Loving for Work: Discourses of Labor in Feminist Sex-work Activism." Feminist Studies40, no. 3 (2014): 693-720. Accessed December 13, 2018.

Dewey, Susan, and Tonia St. Germain. "Women of the Street." 2016. doi:10.18574/nyu/9781479854493.001.0001.

Horton-Stallings, LaMonda. Funk the Erotic: Transaesthetics and Black Sexual Cultures. Urbana, Chicago: University of Illinois Press, 2015.

*originally posted on Patreon

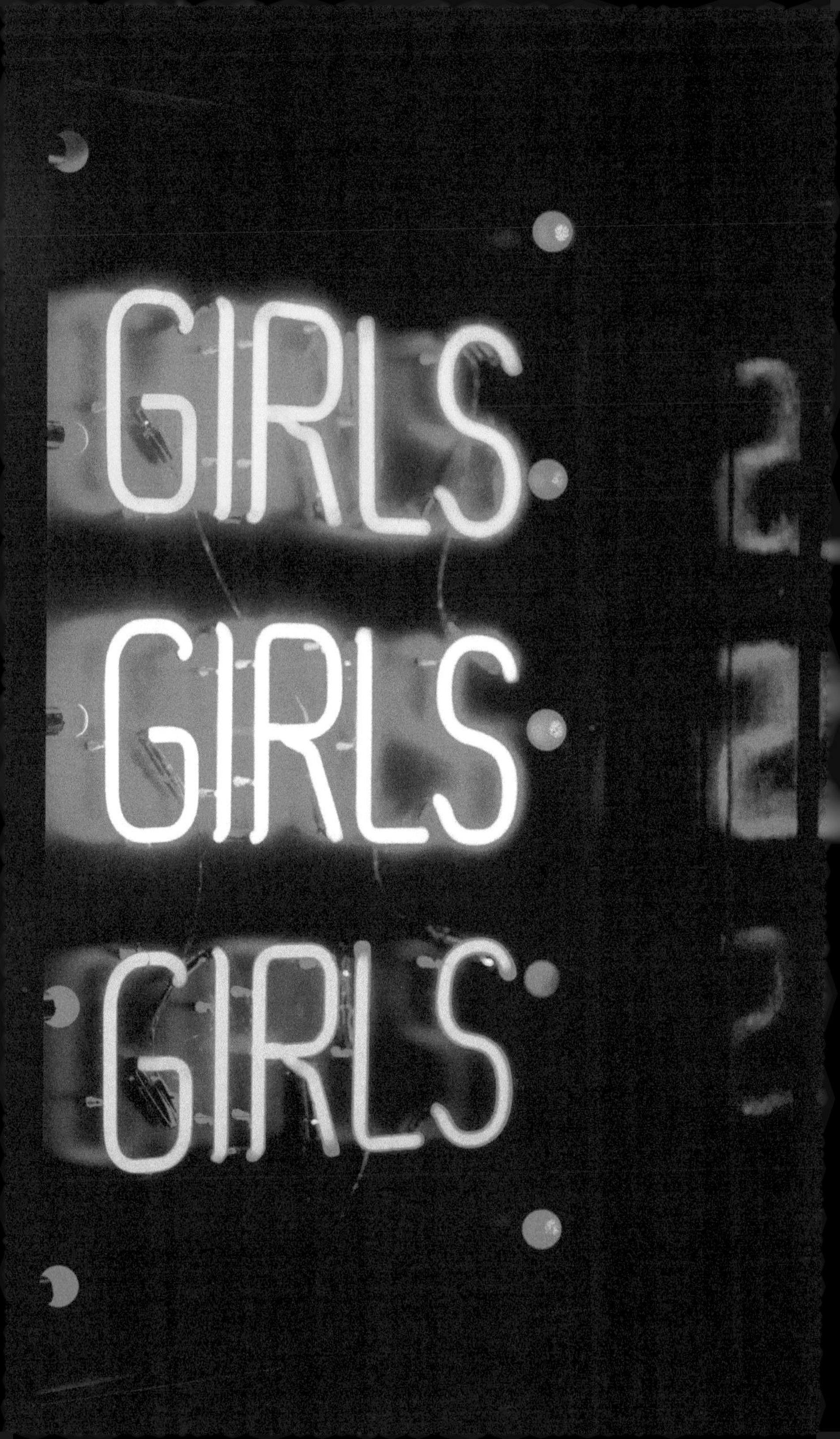
GIRLS
GIRLS
GIRLS

TWITTER THREADS #9, 10, &, 11: ON VOTING AND SEX WORK AS A "SINGLE ISSUE"

I. CONTINUING MY CRITIQUE OF KAMALA HARRIS' ENDORSE-MENT OF THE NORDIC MODEL UNDER THE GUISE OF PRO-TECTING SEX WORKERS AND CHILDREN.

4 THIRD, TOO MANY OF YOU ARE WILLING TO GRANT KAMALA AND OTHERS THE BOD AND I THINK YOU UNDERESTIMATE THE WILLFUL IGNORANCE AND STIGMA AROUND EROTIC LABOR AND A HOST OF OTHER THINGS. SO TODAY I WANT Y'ALL TO THINK ABOUT THE FACT THAT THEY ARE DESCRIBING US AS "SINGLE ISSUE VOTERS."

5 THINK ABOUT THAT. SEX WORKERS ARE SEEN AS "SINGLE ISSUE VOTERS." SO WHAT DO THEY DO? THEY ATTACK THAT *SINGLE ISSUE* THEREBY PROVING THAT THEY DON'T KNOW SHIT ABOUT SEX WORKER POLITICS. BECAUSE MOST OF US ARE ALSO ATTACKING HARRIS POLITICS AROUND INCARCERATION AS WELL.

6 WE AIN'T JUST DISCUSSING SEX WORK AS A SOLITARY ISSUE OVER HERE. WE'RE DISCUSSING POVERTY, HOMELESSNESS, BLACK AND BROWN QUEER AND TRANS ISSUES, ADDICTION, PRISON ABOLITION, IMMIGRATION, ADOPTION/FOS-TER CARE/CPS-- ALL OF THESE COMMUNITIES/ISSUES INTERSECT HEAVILY WITH SEX WORK.

7 CATEGORIZING US AS "SINGLE-ISSUE" FEELS PURPOSEFUL, IT FEELS LIKE DELIBERATE ERASURE OF US IN SEVERAL OTHER ARENAS WHO HAVE BEEN SPEAK-ING, WRITING, AND ORGANIZING. IF Y'ALL THINK A FEW CHOICE WORDS ABOUT DECRIMINALIZATION ARE GONNA SWAY ME, YOU'RE MISTAKEN.

II. AFTER A DEBATE WITH A WHITE LIBERAL ON THE VALIDITY OF NOT VOTING FOR PRESIDENT AKA "THE LESSER OF TWO EVILS."

1 I KNOW THAT SOON THE SEASON WILL COME WHERE PEOPLE WHO ARE LOOKING FOR SOMEONE TO BLAME FOR WHY THIS COUNTRY CONTINUES TO BE RACIST, MISOGYNIST, ETC. WILL BLAME NON-VOTERS, CONSCIENTIOUS OBJEC-TORS OR NOT. I WANNA REMIND FOLKS THAT NOT VOTING IS A VALID CHOICE.

2 I WILL NOT VOTE FOR SOMEONE IF THEY DO NOT REPRESENT MY INTERESTS. ALL OF THE ISSUES THAT ARE IMPORTANT FOR ME ARE CONNECTED. SEX WORK IS NOT A SINGLE ISSUE. MY POLITICS AROUND SEX WORK TOUCH ON A VARIETY OF ISSUES: ABLEISM, SEXISM, GLOBAL AND LOCAL POVERTY, INFORMAL LABOR, ETC.

3 IF NONE OF THE CANDIDATES REPRESENT MY INTERESTS-- REMEMBER I AM AN INFORMED BLACK AMERICAN WOMAN WHO IS POOR AND DESCENDED FROM SLAVES, WHO IS EDUCATED AND UN-DEGREED AND ENGAGES IN EROTIC LABOR AND IS A BIOETHICIST-- I WILL NOT VOTE. THIS IS A POLITICALLY SOUND POSI-TION.

4 I PARTICIPATE IN MY COMMUNITY. I'M HOPING TO ORGANIZE MORE LOCALLY. I MAY OR MAY NOT GO BACK TO VOTING LOCALLY, BECAUSE I BELIEVE THAT WE MIGHT HAVE THE ABILITY TO SHIFT A LOT ON THE STATE LEVEL AND I AM INSPIRED BY NYC AND @DECRIMNY.

I'M POOR & BLACK & I KNOW HOW POLITICS WORK.

5 MY GRAMMA WORKED THE POLLS. BLACK WOMEN WOULD HAVE CARRIED HILLARY TO VICTORY WITH THE HELP OF WHITE WOMEN HAD THEY NOT HAVE BEEN... WHITE. NON-VOTERS ARE NOT TO BLAME FOR TRUMP'S VICTORY. WHITE PEOPLE ARE TO BLAME. REMEMBER THAT BEFORE YOU CHASTISE BW ABOUT RESPONSIBILITY.

6 WE WERE POOR AND WORKING CLASS UNDER CLINTON AND BUSH. I WAS POOR AND VOTED UNDER OBAMA, TWICE. I AM POOR NOW. I'M BLACK AND I, LIKE MANY BLACK PEOPLE HAVE WATCHED POLITICIANS COME AND GO. I HAVE CONTINUED TO PUSH FOR JUSTICE. I HAVE STAYED INFORMED. AND YOU WILL NOT SHAME ME.

7 I MAY VOTE THIS COMING ELECTION. IT'S REALLY NONE OF YOUR BUSINESS BUT POLITICS IS PART OF MY LIFE. I ENCOURAGE YOU TO REDIRECT THE ENER-GY YOU WASTE ON CHASITSING NON-VOTERS TOWARD RACIST/SEXIST WHITE LIBERALS AND CENTRISTS, ESP WHITE VOTERS. PUSH *THEM* TO DO WHAT IS RIGHT.

III. ON USING CHILDREN AS A DOG WHISTLE IN THE FIGHT FOR BODILY/SEXUAL AUTONOMY

1 THE REAL REASON WHITE MEN STARTED FEARMONGERING AND CONCERN TROLLING ABOUT SEX TRAFFICKING WAS TO CONTROL WHITE WOMEN'S SEXUALITY, NOT BECAUSE THEY ACTUALLY GAF ABOUT THE SO-CALLED MILLIONS OF TRAFFICKED CHILDREN. THE SYSTEMS WOULDNT BE THE WAY THEY ARE IF Y'ALL CARED ABOUT KIDS.

2 CHILDREN ARE JUST A PAWN FOR THESE PEOPLE, WHO DON'T CARE TO BE INFORMED OR USE REAL STATISTICS. UNFORTUNATELY, WITH THE HELP OF (MAINLY) WHITE WOMEN, MANY OF WHOM CLAIM TO BE FEMINISTS, THEY HAVE BEEN SUCCESSFUL IN THEIR ATTEMPS TO SUPRESS AND CRIMINALIZE ADULT EROTIC LABORERS.

3 SEX WORKERS CARE ABOUT CHILDREN. MANY OF US ARE PARENTS. MANY OF THE LAWS THAT POLITICIANS HAVE DRAFTED HAVE ACTUALLY PLACED TEENS WHO TRADE SEX IN A POSITION OF EITHER BEING CRIMINALS OR OSTRACIZED FROM REAL SUPPORT. WE CAN'T HELP TEENS WITHOUT FEAR OF BEING LABELED TRAFFICKERS.

4 PEOPLE AGAINST TRAFFICKING WOULD BE ABLE TO HELP TEENS IF THEY 1) LISTENED TO ACTUAL TEENS, 2) LISTENED TO EROTIC LABORERS, & 3) STOPPED CRIMINALIZING PEOPLE FOR TRADING SEX. BUT THEY REFUSE TO LISTEN AND RELY ON FAULTY, BIASED DATA. I HAVE CONCLUDED THAT THEY DON'T WANNA HELP.

5 SINCE WHEN HAS OFFERING ASSISTANCE (HELP) EVER BEEN PRODUCTIVE IF YOU DON'T ENGAGE THE PURPORTED PARTY OR SUBJECTS NEEDING ASSISTANCE? SINCE WHEN HAS THAT EVER "PROTECTED" ANYONE? NO. WHAT Y'ALL WANT TO DO IS *CONTROL* PEOPLE. THAT IS WHY OUR OPINIONS ARE IRRELEVANT TO YOU.

6 Y'ALL CONTINUE TO TELL US TO GET INVOLVED IN POLITICS AND BE ACTIVE CITI-ZENS AND VOTE, BUT YOU DON'T ENGAGE US OR CENTER OUR ISSUES, YOU CALL US "SINGLE ISSUE VOTERS." YOU CLAIM WE ARE IMMATURE OR IGNORANT WHEN WE DON'T VOTE, AND THEN YOU DRAFT LAWS WITHOUT OUR INPUT

ANYWAY.

7 IMAGINE IF SOMEONE SAID "RACE IS A SINGLE ISSUE." OH WAIT BUT THAT'S
LITERALLY HOW THE AMERICAN POLITICS SYSTEM ENAGES PEOPLE'S RIGHTS.
BECAUSE POLITICS IS A GAME AND PEOPLE'S "SINGLE ISSUES"-- MANY OF
WHICH AFFECT THEIR HEALTH, RIGHTS, AND ECONOMIC WELL-BEING-- CAN
ALWAYS WAIT.

8 IMAGINE SOMEONE ENGAGING YOUR POLITICAL ISSUES AS IF YOUR FUCKING
LIVELIHOOD IS A DAMN CHESS MATCH. THAT'S WHAT IT FEELS LIKE TO BE A
POOR BLACK EROTIC LABORER AND CREATIVE. MY "WAIT AND SEE" IS FULL OF
TREPIDATION. THEIR "WAIT AND SEE" IS A GAME.

TWITTER THREAD #12, 13, & 14: A "POOR ASS SEX WORKER"

1 Being poor means constantly being asked to give up everything you want out of life just to get by financially to escape the shame of being poor because poor in this society is a personal embarrassment and if you aren't working yourself to death to avoid that are you even trying?

2 Poverty is rendered as your own personal failure. Poor people are told to give up homeschooling their children, to put every want, need, and desire on hold, We're told, when we protest, that we are being unrealistic. "You must not want it hard enough."

3 The wanting, the needing, the working to get up from under the thumb of capitalism just enough to give our children enough becomes a weighing, a measure of lesser evils. We are blamed for not offering them more. We are blamed when we sacrifice to give them more.

4 We send our kids to public school and are blamed for it, because

public schools are terrible. When we attempt to homeschool and are told not to complain because we have the choice to send them to public school, we are *choosing* hardship.

5 We panhandle online. We post cash links for bare and basic necessities and are publicly embarassed. We must be unfit parents, to have laid our shame so bare online for everyone to see. Poverty is a secret, making other people see it is rude.

6 Poor people aren't allowed criteria/preference. We're not allowed frivolity. We're told to be realistic. We're not seen as trustworthy or honest. Hence why our cash links are fodder for harassment & entertainment. You're poor, they say. You clearly don't know how to handle money.

7 Poor people are infantilized and condescended to, with subpar govt job programs and shitty wages that no one could possibly live on. And then folks sit online and trash McDonald's jobs and retail. When we complain about conditions the solution is: "Just get a better job."

8 I think all the time about having an entire podcast made about me being a poor ass sex worker. I think about how even other sex workers have said: "How could you not be making money?" As if the energy/hours to manage multiple businesses at once and a child doesn't often run out.

9 Poverty, hell capitalism, is demoralizing af. I spend evenings talking with my partner, discussing what we can do to mitigate the weight on me at home, what can we sacrifice. Nothing is settled. Because the money has to be made and bills have to be paid.

10 I did not ask for financial advice anywhere on this thread, nor did I say i was having simple money problems or don't have my shit together. I know how to manage money. I just don't have a lot of it, nor a lot of free/leisure time. Don't give me unasked for suggestions. TY

(11) I added a "summary" after someone suggested a money management book to me and told me that I should work on changing my mindset, in the replies of this tweet:

1 I don't have a cycle. Poverty in and of itself is or can be cyclical. I'm a writer. I homeschool my son and live frugally. I'm married and my partner works long hours. Ends are met. Planning to "get out of poverty" has been an ongoing affair. It is not because of my mindset.

2 My mindset isn't the issue & this is what is being attacked in the thread. This idea that there are so many easy routes out. I produce my own content. I almost always have. I'm a saver but have nothing extra. I am also a planner. My mindset is not the issue. Capitalism is.

THE NEXT DAY MY REPLIES WERE FULL OF BULLSHIT AND I RESPONDED WITH TWO THREADS:

(12) Connecting this tangent. I'm just so angry today. Insomnia has me, and the bills are coming due.

5 When poor people have standards and set them, folks who feel they know better (obvs we are ignorant and poor, what do we know about what we need?) come thru and try to make us lower our standards, just like men who ask "is this a date" twice a year on Twitter.

6 It's like: I said what I wanted. You can either give me the help I need, or you can get out my way. But what folks like to do is see if they can get you to change your criteria. If not, they brand you a scammer or denigrate you. Your poverty makes them uncomfy. It could be them.

7 Every time someone living above the poverty line sees a poor they cover their noses (figuratively) lest they themselves catch

the poor. Because poverty is a disease to be eradicated for these middle-class aspirants.

8 Folks will literally do *anything* to avoid actually seeing or hearing poor people; cities have disappeared homeless people like they are pollution, people litter. "We don't want that in our city." "If you see a tent, report it." Alluh this shit is connected. Disappear, they say.

I DID ANOTHER THREAD LATER THAT DAY:

1 Stop talking to poor people about changing our mindset. Stop putting a cap on how many kids we can have, or what kinds of clothes we should be wearing. Stop insinuating that somehow our poverty is our fault. Most rich folk ain't do shit but be born rich. Small choices my ass.

Quoted tweet deleted: https://twitter.com/lavar_se/status/1155512470485835776

2 Honestly the fact that y'all truly believe that it is okay to tell poor people that they are not allowed to indulge themselves and frame our desire for trendy or nice things as "stupidity" speaks for itself. "How are you homeless with a cellphone?"-ass clowns.

3 My gramma once made a comment like this. "Look at that ngga. Homeless but got enough money for cigarettes. They be lyin." Ma'am. Loosies are a dollar. Tell me how giving up cigarettes is gonna get this homeless vet a house? STOP IT.

4 Life is not just about needs. I want beautiful things but because I'm poor y'all don't think I deserve it. Poor people's poverty, lack of where-withal, and/or homelessness is not a mark of our irresponsibility or needing to make better "small choices."

5 Why I gotta have an ugly sofa, ugly shoes, and no car? As punishment for being poor right? But my ONLY CHILD almost

SEVEN. I'm a saver, always have been. I was looking up Roth IRAs when I was 19, I knew I'd never work a 9-5. But I don't GOT nothin to save.

6 Just say poor people don't deserve nice things. Say that you think having money is indicative of your value, deserving-ness, and intelli-gence. Because even if I scrimped & saved for the nice sofa I want y'all will still tell me I should've saved it or paid some bills.

7 I could've saved for two years to buy the exact sofa that I want, a goldenrod/mustard yellow Chesterfield. And the moment y'all look at my sofa y'all gon say "That's why you poor now!" or 'You should've saved that money." Y'all want poor people living a joyless life.

8 The notion that poor people shouldn't have children is a eugenics based argument that has been used againt black and brown people for decades. We, veterans, addicts, and LGBTQ folks generally make up a good amount of the poor in america.

Quoted tweet deleted: https://twitter.com/lavar_se/status/1155626455562424321?s=19

poor ass sex worker tweets:

thotscholar. (2019, July 27). Being poor means…. [Tweet]. https://twitter.com/ thotscholar/status/1155245465396494337
thotscholar. (2019, July 28). Connecting this tangent… [Tweet]. https://twitter. com/thotscholar/status/1155368125635977216
thotscholar. (2019, July 28). Folks will literally do… [Tweet]. https://twitter.com/ thotscholar/status/1155363591375282182
thotscholar. (2019, July 28). Stop talking to poor people[…] [Tweet]. https://twitter.com/thotscholar/status/1155517154118262784

POVERTY AND MORALITY

These threads on poverty reminded me of an older thread, so I decided to include it here. There's a lotta people who think that having children while in poverty is immoral which should reasonably lead them to con-clude that poverty itself (and the systems which beget it) is immoral, but instead leads them to declare that poor people shouldn't be having kids at all. This is likely because we are taught (in American) culture that our poverty is different from other countries. I remember being told as a child that castes (In India) were *vastly* different than social classes, and that I should not compare the two. I was ten or eleven when a teacher told me that. I recognized that many people in America stayed poor, particularly black and brown people. I was told that poverty was a symbol of sin, of lack of will, of lack of skill/ingeniousness. In short, I was taught that poverty=immoral. Most American children are taught indirectly via media, Christianity, etc. that impoverished people are immoral. Their habits and pleasures are "low." They are causing themselves to stay in poverty. They don't wanna be better. I was given The Parable of Talents as an example.

Poverty is the problem, not our existence. Capitalism is the problem, not our supposed inability to "win" it. People posit the notion of "just don't have kids" as if we are not animals driven to procreate, not just out of self-centeredness, but so that our cultures continue. They also lean on the assumption that poverty is (supposed to be) temporary. Since poverty is temporary, anyone who remains impover-ished is a failure, lazy, etc. Nevermind a recession, forget about cyclical poverty and systemic racism. Erebody grindin'. Erebody a potential entrepreneur, and so on. The fact that there's a large amount of Black folks that think like this is disappointing for me, but not surprising.

Christianity tells us that if we do right, if we are virtuous, we will be delivered from our suffering. So, the logic follows that if we pray hard enough, if we are "good," our life will improve. But poor Black folk got questions. So we ask why we continue to be broke, what the deal? And the pastors say, Well ya gotta do summa the work ya'self. Obviously, right? And so it goes, we are told that God gives us the tools. So if you broke what you doing? Sinnin, prolly.

This view of poverty leaves little room for empathy for poor folks who have children, especially panhandlers who may or may not be home-less, because it equates our procreation to mere selfishness and not an animal imperative to continue the human race, and our respective cultures. People have children to give birth to the future, whatever that may be. Are rich people's children gonna be the ones to ensure a fair and equal future? Are they gonna be the ones to redistribute wealth and eradicate poverty? Since that hasn't happened yet, I'm assuming the answer is no. It is those of us who were born into poverty or black-ness, or whatever form of inequality or systemic oppression you can think of, who agitate for change.

That is not to say that, on a personal level, we don't worry about the wellbeing of our children. But to say that poor people should abstain from having children entirely? That is speaking us into un-existence. When you say that the solution to keeping children from being born into poverty is to just not have children, you are placing the responsibility for poverty on the shoulders of the op-pressed. It's like saying if Black people don't want their children to be oppressed, they should just not have children. Why is it the responsibility of the oppressed to avoid oppression? Why should the automatic solution to street harass-ment and rape be to "cover up" and "carry a weapon" instead of to teach boys better and protect victims who retaliate against or name their assaulters?

We have this way of using children as a conversation stopper. It keeps us from exploring logical solutions. I think a certain part of us is conditioned to accept the norms we've been socialized into. And a lot of folks see children as these beacons of unsullied inno-cence, instead of the fleshly, worldy human beings they become as soon as they are squeezed into the world. So people say "think about the children," when they are decrying "sex trafficking" yet targeting adult erotic laborers. "Think about the children," when we are debating the existence of prisons. It's not because they actually care about children-- our laws don't reflect that. It's because children are symbolic. Everybody is supposed to care about children, because "children are our future." If children are the future and y'all want poor people to stop having chil-dren, what does that mean for our future? Does our ceasing to exist mean poverty will cease? Is the eradication of poor people gonna end wealth-hoarding? Will it repair the detrimental effects of global capi-talism, war, and genocide? Or is poor people not having children a bandaid, a convenient solution to the millions (billions?) of people suffering worldwide.

The sin is not poor people having children. The sin is using children you don't care about anyway to promote classism and justify an entire demographic's social death.

TWITTER THREAD #15

1 MONEY AND INTIMACY GO HAND IN HAND.

2 I LOVE AMALIA CABEZAS WORK AROUND WHAT SHE CALLS "SEXUAL–AFFECTIVE" RELATIONSHIPS. IT REALLY GAVE ME SOME MUCH NEEDED LANGUAGE TO ARTICULATE MY PERSPECTIVE ON THIS ISSUE SOME FOLKS HAVE WITH MIXING INTIMACY/SEX WITH MONEY. (WHICH IS WHAT MARRIAGE IS.)

3 IT IS STRANGE (THOUGH NOT UNEXPECTED) THAT MANY PEOPLE THINK MONEY IS "DIRTY" AND SULLIES INTIMACY. IN MY EXPERIENCE, BOTH WITH EROTIC LABOR AND WITH MARRIAGE AND ROMANTIC RELATIONSHIPS, MONEY ONLY ENHANCED THE CONNECTION. THIS ALSO HOLDS TRUE IN FAMILIAL RELATIONSHIPS.

4 MONEY IS AN OFFERING. OF SOLIDARITY, OF CARE. AND CARE IS AN IMPORTANT PART OF INTIMACY, IS IT NOT? SO IT PUZZLES ME THAT I CONSTANTLY ENCOUNTER PEOPLE WHO BELIEVE MONEY MAKES THE INTIMACY "FORCED." ESPECIALLY BLACK FOLKS WHO GREW UP WITH SONGS LIKE BILLS, BILLS, BILLS.

5 IT'S CLEAR THAT MANY MARGINALIZED WOMEN LARGELY HAVE AN UNDERSTANDING OF SEXUAL– AFFECTIVE RELATIONSHIPS AND HOW THAT MONETARY SOLIDARITY IS KEY TO A BENEFICIAL CONNECTION BETWEEN PEOPLE. SENDING MONEY TO FAMILY. MEN SENDING MONEY TO WOMEN/EROTIC LABORERS. IT'S A FORM OF CARE.

6 SENDING MONEY IS NOT REVOLUTIONARY, NOR IS IT RADICALLY DISRUPTING THE STATUS QUO, AS SOME HAVE CLAIMED. BUT IT IS A LOVE/CARE LANGUAGE. THE ACTUAL "DIRTY" THING IS DENYING THIS CARE BASED ON PURITANICAL (SEXIST) VALUES ABOUT MONEY+INTIMACY. CARE

HEIGHTENS INTIMACY.

7 THIS IS WHAT EROTIC LABORERS MEAN WHEN WE TALK ABOUT OUR RELATIONSHIPS WITH CERTAIN CLIENTS, AKA "REGULARS." THIS ISN'T ABOUT "HUMANIZING" CLIENTS. THIS IS ABOUT THE ASSESSMENT THAT CERTAIN KINDS OF INTIMACY ARE SOMEHOW EXEMPT FROM THIS BASIC RULE OF GIVE AND TAKE.

8 I TRULY BELIEVE THAT MOST PEOPLE'S, PARTICULARLY CIS MEN'S, ISSUE WITH "PAYING FOR SEX" COMES DOWN TO THEIR FEELING THAT ONE CAN ACTUALLY SEPARATE SEX FROM INTIMACY. BUT SEX--TOUCH--IS A FORM OF INTI-MACY, AND INTIMACY HAPPENS ON VARIOUS LEVELS. ALL OF THIS COMES DOWN TO CARE.

9 ALSO IT SHOULDN'T BE LEFT UNSAID THAT CARE WORK-- WHICH IS WHAT MANY FORMS OF EROTIC LABOR ARE-- IS MAINLY PERFORMED BY WOMEN AND FEMININE PEOPLE, AND THUS IS LARGELY DEVALUED AS A WHOLE. INTERROGATE THE SEXISM EMBEDDED IN "PAYING FOR SEX IS DEGRADING." FOR WHOMST?

10 HOW IS IT THAT MONETARY EXCHANGE SULLIES INTIMACY WHEN IT COMES TO TOUCH/SEX BUT NOT WHEN YOUR MOM PUTS MONEY IN YOUR BANK ACCOUNT? WHY DOES MONEY RUIN SEXUAL INTIMACY BUT NOT MY RELATIONSHIP WITH MY SISTER WHEN SHE SENDS ME $100 BECAUSE I NEED IT?

11 ANYWAY. THE MATHS ARE THIS:

MONEY/ITEMS+INTIMACY=CARE/LOVE/SOLIDARITY IS (GREATER THAN) _____ "FOR FREE"

MY MOM SENT ME MONEY AND CARED FOR MY KID. I HELPED HER PUT HER WASHER AND DRYER IN.
MONEY ENSURES A CLOSE TO EVEN EXCHANGE WHEN IT

COMES TO VARIOUS FORMS OF CARE WORK AND LABOR.

12 **MUCH OF THIS ALSO APPLIES TO CHILD SUPPORT. A LOT OF THE MENS HAVE A PROBLEM WITH SEEING MONEY AS A FORM OF CARE. MY KID'S BIO-DAD CONTINUES TO PROCLAIM HIS UNDYING LOVE FOR ME AND MY SON BUT MY POCKETS BEG TO DIFFER.

SOURCE: THOTSCHOLAR. (2019, JUNE 15). MONEY AND INTIMACY GO HAND IN HAND [TWEET]. HTTPS://TWITTER.COM/THOTSCHOLAR/STATUS/1139772567257059328

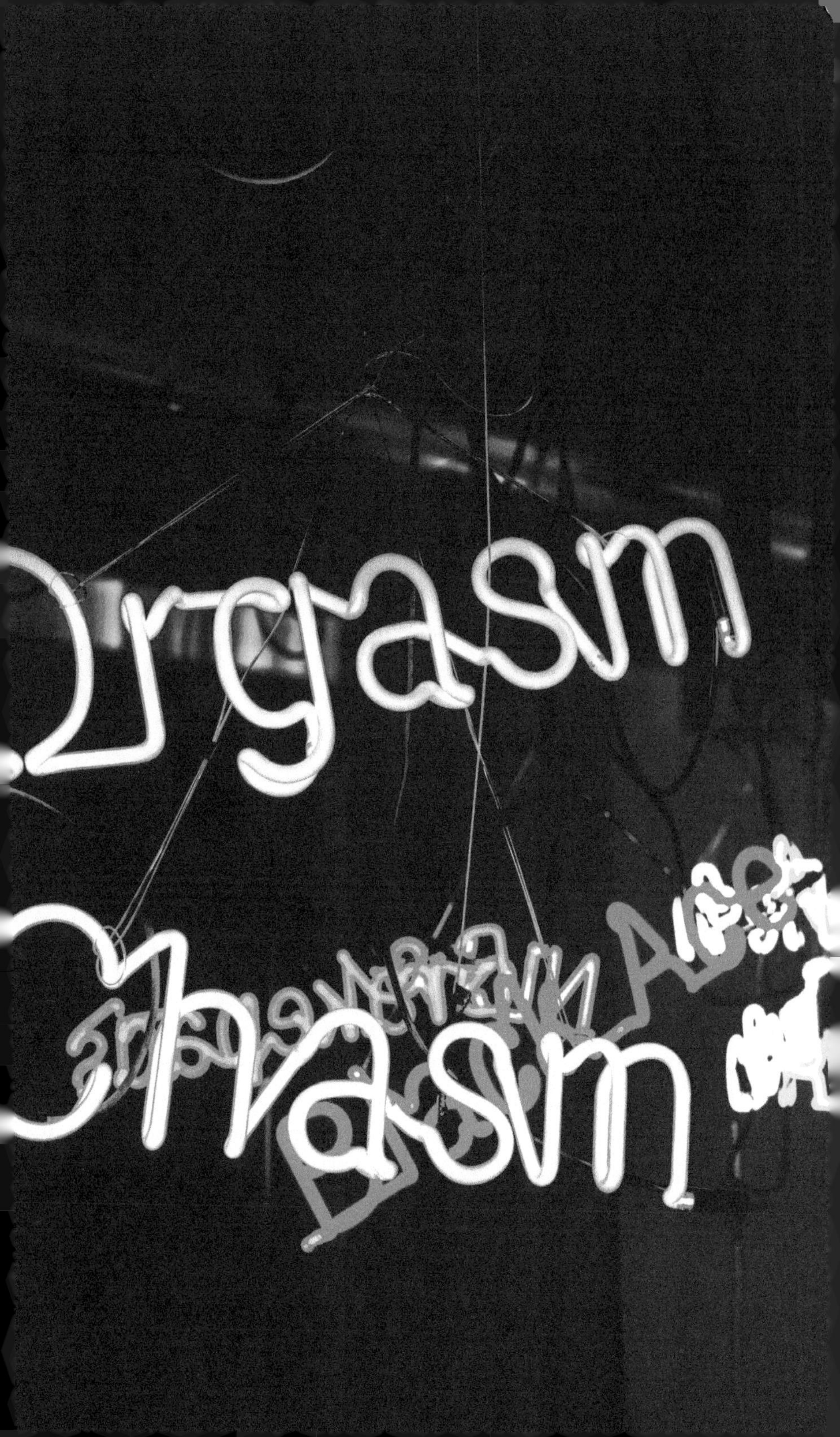
Orgasm
Orgasm

PROHEAUX[2] POLITICS VS. MAINSTREAM SEX POSITIVITY:
BEYOND "HOE IS LIFE"

** THIS WAS ORIGINALLY COMMISSIONED BY FOR HARRIET OFF A TWITTER THREAD I WROTE SOMETIME IN 2017 OR 2018, BUT WAS NEVER PUBLISHED. AFTER TWO ROUNDS OF EDITS, I DIDN'T HEAR BACK FROM THE EDITOR. A BIT AFTER THAT, SHE TOLD ME SHE HAD FORGOT-TEN ME. I WAS NOT PAID A KILL FEE OR COMPENSATED FOR MY TIME. THIS IS A REVISED VERSION OF "EXAMINING PROHEAUX POLITICS & THE NOUVEAU THOT AESTHETIC"

In this Fourth Wave of Black feminism, a resurgence of sexual liberation politics has emerged. Combined with pleasure activism, Black Lives Matter, indigenous spirituality, globalization, and trans rights activism , a new hoe aesthetic has emerged. The current pop culture trends are #intersectionalfeminist, "pro hoe," and #misandry, which is not feminism but is extremely cathartic and, I think, connected to the rise of financial domination. Financial domination, or findom, is a previously little-known form of domination fetish work where the dominatrix collects subs (submissives), sometimes referred to as "money slaves," who give them money for the pleasure of being "drained," or some-

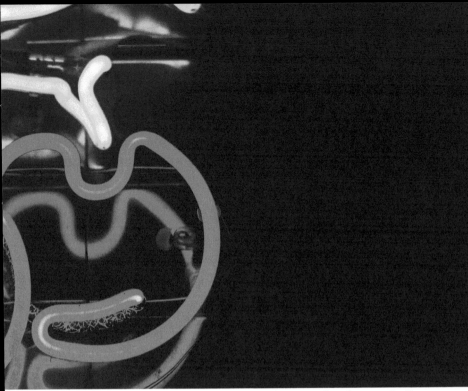

times for other specific, related kinks or fetishes. Findom certain kinks, and erotic labor terminology, are crossing over into the mainstream cultural lexicon. Sex positive feminists love transgressive sexuality just like anyone else. Hoe/slut chic is the new wave.

Now, when I scroll through my timeline, I often see Black women asking for advice on sugaring (being a sugar baby) or counseling other women on the peril or shame of "giving it away for free" to thankless cishet men. There is a strange correlation between these women and the women who advocate marrying up to better our line. Nobody wants be a sex worker, but everybody wants to be a sex worker. Financial domination and sugaring seem to have replaced exotic dancing as the most glamorized sex work professions by virtue of the internet, the rise of the Instagram model/reality TV star and, in the case of findomming, lack of actual physical contact. Many women now think of these profes-sions as fringe acceptable, like BDSM post-50 Shades of Gray. Reality TV stars and celebrities have actually replaced (or displaced) the supermodel. Being or claiming to be or have been a sex worker online now gives one a certain amount of edge. Even saying you "dabbled" will get you some modicum of proheaux (also spelled "pro hoe") legitimacy. There is an air of dirty glamour afforded to our much-maligned profession. It is illegitimate and dangerous, yet empowering and exciting, all at once.

Yet, erotic laborers are still viewed as throwaways, not a representation of real women, and nothing like what we'd want our daughters to aspire to. Erotic labor is seen as skills-light and easy, even lazy, because of the ease of entry into the trade. Like most trades, it is denigrated and classed, unless you are making a ton of money doing it. If not, you are relegated to the dregs of society, and because all men want sex and "pussy rules the world" (insert the myth of cis women's pussy power) if you are failing it is your own fault, racism, cissexism, and other forms of oppression and beauty standards notwithstanding. All of the latter are looked at as excuses. Cis men's desire to fuck you is paramount to success as an erotic laborer, and if you failed at that then there must be something fundamentally wrong with you. It's not as if men are subject to the same socialization as we are, not as if our clients are mostly racist cis white men.

Still, I have witnessed an uptick in women who want to pick my brain on how to find a Sugar Daddy or get into camming. They toss these words around casually and talk about finessing men for meals and bills. Whore hierarchy: If you haven't finessed a car or a house out of a man, are you even doing it right? Or: Why have sex for things when you could just get cash? When I break everything down (from "survival sex work" to income inequality), or attempt to inject some realism about the misogynoir and risk involved in a socially stigmatized sales job based on one's looks and charisma and cis men's consumption of you, I am accused of behaving like a gatekeeper. I'm trying to keep them from the fun. I'm ruining the fantasy.

This shift is interesting considering Black women have a very different history with our bodies and sexuality than many nonblack women. Recently there's been a wave of seemingly pro-hoe politics that I thought would shift the focus from individual sexual politics a la "hoe is life" to a more collective stance leaning toward a liberating body politic, and that perhaps it would lead to a focus on another, widely varied group (erotic laborers) affected by the criminalization of deviant bodies and the effect of these white/male dominated institutions on them. However, I have mostly found the focus to be skewed toward cis women's personal sexual liberation via pleasure activism and navigating Capitalism — both of which are important. But just as important, if not more, are de-criminalization/destigmatization of erotic labor and trans bodies, HIV+ education, reproductive justice and access to healthcare (birth control, hormones, etc.) — and all of these issues are highly racialized as well as gendered. And they are all connected.

I am aware that there are women who both maintain their own personal sexual freedom and manage to center those who are affected by the aforementioned issues. I am one. But I have a feeling women like myself are in the minority — and that many of us who do address both are marginalized and fit these categories. Although sexual liberation and polyamory have risen in popularity, unsurprisingly queer/trans rights and sex worker rights continue to take a political backseat. Both white women and liberal Black feminists/womanists tend to forget or dismiss erotic laborers and our concerns entirely. "Hoe is life" is just another brand of fuck-me feminism that allows feminists and womanists to engage in choice feminist pleasure praxis without engaging people who fuck for a living. Black cis women, both feminists and nah, continue to hurl misogynoiristic slurs at erotic laborers and side chicks, even as they clamor to try polyamory on for size or "marry up," their idea of surviving under capitalism. What erotic laborers want is too radical. What if we fuck their men? It's not surprising that this brand of feminism (if you want to call it that) also tends to be anti-trans— they want to decide who is considered a "real woman" and trans women and erotic laborers (who are automatically breaking "girl code") fall decidedly outside of that category. Similarly, many of these same women hold rigid ideas of what a "real man" is, and a man who fucks or is attracted to trans women does not fit the mold. Cis women are highly insecure about their place in the culture, afraid whores and trans women will take their spot. This is probably part of the reason behind the resurgence in pussy-centric and divine-goddess spirituality.

Many Black women separate the erotic from the "pornographic" and consider all forms of erotic labor to be exploitative. I find this curious considering erotic labor is something that is done in the sex trade as well as in heterosexual pairings. The erotic is not separate from the pornographic—all pleasure is excessive or offensive to somebody. Rather, erotic labor in the sex trade reflects both fantasy and reality. Fantasy-made-reality and reality-made-fantasy can both be expressions of eroticism. Toeing the line of the 'all women are whores' adage that "marry up" feminists peddle on social media like prosperity gospel preachers, I want people to understand that all feminized labor is connected—As in any of the multitude of industries based in physical appearance (such as modeling, film, and certain sports), racism, fetishism, and fatphobia are compounded in the erotic labor industry. All labor is skewed/affected by misogyny/-noir and racism, among other strutural inequalities. Getting a man to pay your bills is not so much liberation as it is harm reduction— a way to navigate a sexist society and ease the burden of economic inequality.

Demands for gender-based reparations via personal transactions (or donations) have been centered in this movement toward a personal liberation: take the waning popularity of the GiveYourMoneytoWomen findom hashtag, another example of unsustainable capitalism-centered (white/popular) feminism, which forgoes a reality-based intersectional lens in favor of centering on gender and casual misandry, race and economics be damned. In the same way, "marry up" feminists choose to ignore or gloss over key issues surrounding classism and racism in order to make their viewpoint fit. Similarly, "hoe is life" is a trend that is focused on Black women's (and those nonblack women who choose to co-opt it) sexual liberation, but often falls short of supporting erotic laborer's fight for reproductive/sexual justice and liberation.

In her essay "Sex Positive: Feminism, Queer Theory, and the Politics of Transgression," Elisa Glick critiqued this trend of liberatory subversive sexuality and also the lack of self-awareness mainstream sex positive feminists tend to have and their inadequate response when confronted with anti-racist and anti-capitalist critiques. Said Glick:

> "By creating a climate in which self-transformation is equated with social transformation, the new identity politics has valorized a politics of lifestyle, a personal politics that is centered upon who we are — how we dress or get off — that fails to engage with institutionalized systems of domination." In lay people's terms, this is called "choice feminism."

"Hoe is Life" cannot be our stopping point. Note: I know that it has also become trendy to disparage feminists/womanists for dressing "too feminine" or engaging in stereotypical feminine activites or casual sex. However, that isn't my goal. My goal is that we push even harder for more radical practical theory. I'm moving to replace "sex positivity" with "proheauxism," a theory that centers the multiply marginalized and was created by an erotic laborer (me) who is also impoverished, a parent, queer (bisexual), and an independent scholar and artist. This pro hoe stuff in our Twitter bios is cute, but that alone isn't going to produce the changes we so desperately need. Erotic labor, domestic labor, and other forms of feminized and classed labor, can all be seen as extensions of the systemic exploitation of marginalized people's labor and bodies. To dismantle this, we must move beyond "hoe is life" and start thinking about how to better unite against a government which seeks to control us via legislation of our bodies. Proheauxism seeks to make the connections between erotic labor, reproductive/ sexual justice, womanism, and many other movements against inequality, more apparent. Black cis women can not advocate for liberation for themselves while excluding erotic laborers and trans women. Either hoe is life, or it ain't.

Endnotes

1   There is an erotic laborer now utilizing the phrase "heaux history" after a series of conversations we had about my forthcoming nonfiction project that I told them was meant to center the "heaux histories" of my sex worker siblings. We briefly decided to team up to create a documentary series after I showed them my work. After I paid them for their part in a project that was supposed to link my (established) work to their new idea, our relationship unfortunately lapsed. Bittersweet, but it is still my aim to collect contemporary heaux histories. Just wanna be clear that this is exactly how I phrased my pre-existing idea and that this was how I described my work to this person. Our work is not connected and mine pre-dates theirs.

2   I coined the terms "proheaux womanist/proheauxism" but not "pro-hoe/pro-heaux" which was used colloquially as an extension of "hoe is life" esque politics for some time before.

CPSIA information can be obtained
at www.ICGtesting.com
Printed in the USA
LVHW071403130421
684371LV00022B/1465